Ninja Foodi

Easy-to-Prepare Recipes for You and Your F

CW00996449

Table of Contents

Introduction

Ninja Foodi is the most advanced electric pressure cooker ever. It's a smart, multi-function kitchen appliance that cooks food up to 70% faster than other methods.

Ninja Foodi is an electric pressure cooker with time and temperature control settings, so you can cook anything from beef stew to bolognese sauce without worrying about overcooking it. The integrated thermal sensor constantly adjusts cooking power so that your food stays juicier and more tender.

Ninja Foodi has a large 6.5-quart capacity, so you can fit in family-sized meals like chicken cacciatore and moist turkey breast. It's the perfect size for a family of four or to feed company on the holidays.

The pressure cooker's simple LCD display and interface make it easy to use, whether you are a beginner or pro at pressure cooking. The steamer basket fits in two different positions so you can cook vegetables or steam seafood with your main course.

You can also use Ninja Foodi to sauté food right in the insert for a quick stir-fry or add ingredients and deglaze the insert before using it as a slow cooker.

You can sauté food directly in the insert for stir-fries and fried rice, or use it as a slow cooker that keeps all the flavor of your prep work.

Ninja Foodi is designed to cook food up to 70% faster than other methods like boiling or steaming. The pressure cooker has precision control settings, so you can program in the cooking time and temperature you need for any recipe. It has smart Steam Technology, so it automatically adjusts cooking power for optimal results every time.

Ninja Foodi is easy to use, so you can get dinner on the table fast. The pressure cooker's simple LCD display and interface make it easy to use, whether you are a beginner or pro at pressure cooking.

The recipes contained in this guide will be completely searchable. No more flipping through cookbooks, trying to find the cookbook section that contains the recipe you want.

This book is all about pressure cooking and will provide you with a wide range of pressures that can be used and provides you with recipes to get some great tasting dishes.

Enjoy!

Beginner Ninja Foodi Users Recipes

Coconut Oatmeal

Servings: 6

Prep Time: 25 minutes

Ingredients:

- 250 ml shredded dried coconut flakes
- 750 ml coconut milk
- 750 ml water
- 60 ml psyllium husks
- 125 ml coconut flour
- 7.5 ml vanilla extract
- 2.5 ml cinnamon
- 125 ml granulated stevia

Directions:

1. Add all of the ingredients into the Ninja Foodi and stir together briefly
2. Place the lid on and set the steamer valve to seal. Set the pressure cooker function to 1 minute (it will take about 10 minutes to come to pressure).
3. When the oatmeal is done, do a quick pressure release by opening the steamer valve carefully.
4. Serve while hot

Nutrition: Calories 202, Fat 16g, Carbohydrates 6g, Protein 3g.

Servings: 6

Preparation Time: 15 minutes

Ingredients:

- 375 ml chopped almonds
- 750 ml almond milk
- 450 ml water
- 125 ml psyllium husks
- 7.5 ml vanilla extract
- 2.5 ml cinnamon
- 1.25 ml nutmeg
- 125 ml granulated stevia

Directions:

1. Add all of the ingredients into the Ninja Foodi and stir together briefly
2. Place the lid on and set the steamer valve to seal.
3. Set the pressure cooker function to 1 minute (it will take about 10 minutes to come to pressure).
4. When the oatmeal is done, do a quick pressure release by opening the steamer valve carefully.
5. Serve while hot

Nutrition: Calories 136, Fat 9g, Carbohydrates 3g, Protein 4g.

Servings: 4

Preparation Time: 18 minutes

Ingredients

- 4 eggs

- 60 ml heavy cream

- 85g Cheddar cheese, shredded

- 85g shrimps, peeled, cooked

- 2.5 ml salt

- 125 ml of water

Directions

1. Beat the eggs in the bowl and whisk well.

2. Add heavy cream, salt, and cheese. Str it.

3. Chop the shrimps roughly and add in egg mixture.

4. Pour the egg mixture into the muffin molds.

5. Add water in the pot.

6. Place the muffins molds on the rack.

7. Cover the molds with the foil well.

8. Close the lid and seal it. Cook the bites on High for 12 minutes. (Natural pressure release)

9. Discard the foil from bites and transfer them on the serving plates. Taste it!

Nutrition: Calories 200, Fats 14.6g, Carbohydrates 1.1g, Protein 15.8g.

Servings: 4

Preparation Time: 17 minutes

Ingredients

- 15 ml extra-virgin olive oil
- 450g broccoli, cut into florets
- 450g cauliflower, cut into florets
- 60 ml almond flour
- 450 ml coconut milk
- 2.5 ml ground nutmeg
- Pinch of pepper
- 375 ml shredded Gouda cheese, divided

Directions

1. Pre-heat your Ninja Foodi by setting it to Sauté mode
2. Add olive oil and let it heat up, add broccoli and cauliflower
3. Take a medium bowl stir in almond flour, coconut milk, nutmeg, pepper, 250 ml cheese and add the mixture to your Ninja Foodi
4. Top with 125 ml cheese and lock lid, cook on HIGH pressure for 5 minutes
5. Release pressure naturally over 10 minutes
6. Serve and enjoy!

Nutritional Information (per serving): Calories 373, Fat 32g, Carbohydrates 6g, *Protein 16g.*

Servings: 4

Preparation Time: 15 minutes

Ingredients

- 1 pack, 350g frozen broccoli florets
- 30 ml butter
- salt and pepper as needed
- 8 whole eggs
- 30 ml milk
- 750 ml white cheddar cheese, shredded
- Crushed red pepper, as needed

Directions

1. Add butter and broccoli to your Ninja Foodi
2. Season with salt and pepper according to your taste
3. Set the Ninja to Medium Pressure mode and let it cook for about 10 minutes, covered, making sure to keep stirring the broccoli from time to time
4. Take a medium sized bowl and add crack in the eggs, beat the eggs gently
5. Pour milk into the eggs and give it a nice stir
6. Add the egg mixture into the Ninja (over broccoli) and gently stir, cook for 2 minutes (uncovered)
7. Once the egg has settled in, add cheese and sprinkle red pepper, black pepper, and salt
8. Enjoy with bacon strips if you prefer!

Nutritional Information (per serving): Calories 197, Fat 13g, Carbohydrates 5g, Protein 14g

---

Servings: 2

Preparation Time: 25 minutes

Ingredients

- 5 ml butter
- 5 ml cream cheese
- 15 ml almond flour
- 1 egg, beaten
- 50g Cheddar, grated
- 2.5 ml salt
- 1.25 ml black pepper
- 125 ml water (for cooking on High)

Directions

1. Mix up together the cream cheese, butter, egg, cheese, almond flour, ground black pepper, paprika and salt.

2. Whisk the mixture until smooth. Afterwards, pour 125 ml water in the pot. Insert the rack.

3. Transfer the batter in the prepared muffins molds and place on the rack

4. Cover the muffins with the foil and close the lid.

5. Make sure you seal the lid and cook on PRESSURE mode (High) for 15 minutes

6. Then make the quick pressure release for 5 minutes

7. Chill the muffins little and serve

Nutrition: Calories 203, Fat 17g, Carbohydrates 1.9g, Protein 11.1g

Servings: 3

Preparation Time: 10 minutes

Ingredients

- 6 jalapeno peppers
- 5 ml minced garlic
- 90 ml cream cheese
- 6 bacon strips, chopped, cooked
- 2.5 ml salt
- 30 g ground beef, cooked
- 1.25 ml ground cumin

Directions

1. Trim the ends of the peppers and remove all the seeds from inside.
2. Mix up together the minced garlic, cream cheese, salt, and ground cumin. Add the ground beef and stir well. Add bacon.
3. Fill the peppers with the mixture and transfer on the rack.
4. Lower the air fryer lid and cook the jalapenos for minutes at 185 C.
5. Serve the meal immediately!

Nutrition: Calories 301, Fat 26g, Carbohydrates 3g, Protein 12.9g.

Servings: 2

Preparation Time: 30 minutes

Ingredients

- 50 g asparagus, chopped
- 3 eggs, whisked
- 30 ml almond milk
- 5 ml almond flour
- 2.5 ml salt
- 1.25 ml cayenne pepper
- 15g Parmesan, grated
- 5 ml coconut oil

Directions

1. Preheat the pot on "Sauté/Stear mode.
2. Add coconut oil and chopped asparagus.
3. Sauté the vegetable for 3 minutes.
4. Meanwhile, mix up together the almond milk, whisked, eggs, almond flour, cayenne pepper, and grated cheese.
5. Pour the egg mixture into the pot.
6. Close the lid and seal it. Cook the frittata on High (Pressure mode) for 15 minutes.
7. After this, make a quick pressure release.
8. Lower the air fryer lid and cook the meal at 204 C for 6 minutes more.
9. When the surface of the frittata is crusty enough – finish cooking and serve it!

***Nutrition**: Calories 165, Fat 12.3g, Carbohydrates 3.1g, Protein 11.8g.*

Servings: 2

Preparation Time: 45 minutes

Ingredients

- 450g chicken breast, skinless, boneless
- 5 ml curry paste
- 30 ml butter
- 5 ml cayenne pepper
- 125 ml of water

Directions

1. Rub the chicken breast with the curry paste and place in the pot.
2. Sprinkle the poultry with cayenne pepper and add butter.
3. Pour water in the pot and close the lid. Seal the lid.
4. Set Pressure mode and cook on High for 30 minutes.
5. Then make natural pressure release for 10 minutes.
6. Open the lid and shred the chicken inside the pot with the help of the fork.
7. Then close the lid and sauté the chicken for 5 minutes more.
8. Serve it!

Nutrition: Calories 380, Fat 18.8g, Carbohydrates 1.2g, Protein 48.4g

Servings: 1

Preparation Time: 20 minutes

Ingredients

- 115g mushroom hats
- 4 quail eggs
- 1.25 ml salt
- 2.5 ml ground black pepper
- 5 ml butter, melted

Directions

1. Spread the mushroom hats with the butter inside.
2. Then beat the eggs into the mushroom hats and sprinkle with the ground black pepper and salt.
3. Transfer the mushroom hats on the rack and lower the air fryer lid.
4. Cook the meal at 185 C for 7 minutes.
5. Then check the mushrooms and cook them for 2 minutes more.
6. Serve it!

Nutrition: Calories 118, Fat 8.2g, Carbohydrates 4.6g, Protein 8.4g

Servings: 3

Preparation Time: 22 minutes

Ingredients

- 280g chicken thighs, boneless, skinless
- 5 ml turmeric
- 5 ml chili flakes
- 2.5 ml salt
- 1.25 ml ground nutmeg
- 3.75 ml ground ginger
- 125 ml heavy cream
- 30 ml butter
- 5 ml kosher salt

Directions

1. Preheat Ninja Foodi pot at Sauté/Stear mode for 5 minutes.
2. Toss the butter in the pot and melt it.
3. Add turmeric, chili flakes, salt, and ground nutmeg. Then, add ground ginger and salt. Bring to boil the mixture.
4. Meanwhile, chop the chicken thighs roughly.
5. Transfer the chicken thighs in the pot and cooks for 5 minutes at Sauté mode.
6. After this, add heavy cream and close the lid. Seal the lid. Select Pressure mode and set High pressure
7. Cook it for 6 minutes. Then make a quick pressure release.
8. Chill the cooked chicken bites little and serve!

Nutrition: *Calories 322, Fat 22.3g, Carbohydrates 1.5g, Protein 28g.*

Main Course Components & Full Recipes

Ninja Foodi Turkey Breast

Prep & Cooking time: 1 hour 5 minutes

Serving 4

Ingredients

- 1.3-1.8kg skinless, boneless turkey breast
- 30 ml of maple syrup
- 15 ml of spicy mustard
- 10 ml of cumin
- 5 ml of salt
- 2.5 ml of paprika
- 5 ml of oregano

Directions

1. Coat the meat in rub ingredients and let it marinate for an hour in the fridge. Preheat foodi for about five minutes at 175 C and spray with oil.

2. Then cook the turkey for 25 minutes and wait for 10 minutes before slicing.

Nutrition Values (Per Serving): Calories- Kcal 378 | Fat: 6g | Carbs: 8g | Protein: 74g

Prep & Cooking time: 20 minutes

Serving 14

Ingredients

- 4 chopped hotdogs in 4ths
- 1 60 ml white flour
- 750 ml of cornmeal
- 60 ml white sugar
- 10 ml of baking powder
- 2.5 ml of salt
- 250 ml milk
- 1 egg
- 60 ml of oil
- 125 ml water

Directions

1. Combine all the dry ingredients together then add egg, oil, and milk. In a lightly oiled egg mold, fill each space to half.

2. Chop the hot dog in four pieces and put one piece in the middle of every pocket.

3. Enclose it with foil then place the mold in a pressure cooker trivet and pour water in the base. Cook for nine minutes at high pressure. Then let it sit for 5 minutes and pop them out by flipping the mold.

Nutrition Values (Per Serving): Calories: Kcal 170 | Fat: 7g | Carbs: 21g | Protein: 4g

Prep & Cooking time: 15 minutes

Serving 6

Ingredients

- 6 skinless, boneless, chicken thighs, bite-size chunks
- 60 ml of brown sugar
- 22.5 ml minced garlic
- 125 ml soy sauce
- 15 ml of Worcestershire sauce
- 15 ml of honey
- 1 sliced onion
- 2 diced green onions
- 30 ml of cornstarch
- 125 ml chicken broth
- 60 ml hoisin sauce

Directions

1. Put the chicken and onion together in a pot. In another bowl, add together the rest of the ingredients except for half of the green onions.
2. Then toss it in the pot and coat the chicken. Cook for three minutes at high pressure then switch to sauté. Add cornstarch to the bowl and mix with the liquid from the pot.
3. Add it to the pot and let it thicken for a minute or two.
4. Serve with the tortilla or rice.

Nutrition Values (Per Serving): Calories-Kcal 316 | Fat: 18g | Carbs: 17g | Protein: 19g

Green Pesto A la Beef

Preparation Time: 10 minutes

Cooking Time: 14 minutes

Servings: 4

INGREDIENTS:

- 4 beef (175g) tenderloin steak
- 280g baby spinach, chopped
- 1 litre penne pasta, uncooked
- 1 litre grape tomatoes, halved
- 125 ml walnuts, chopped
- 150 ml pesto
- 125 ml feta cheese, crumbled
- 2.5 ml salt
- 2.5 ml pepper

DIRECTIONS:

1. Prepare the pasta as per the given instructions on the pack
2. Drain and rinse, then keep this pasta aside.
3. Flavor the tenderloin steaks with salt and pepper
4. Preheat Ninja Foodi by pressing the "GRILL" option and setting it to "HIGH" for 7 minutes
5. Once it preheats until you hear a beep, open the lid
6. Place the steaks in the grill grate and cook for 7 minutes
7. Flip it and cook for 7 minutes
8. Take a bowl and toss the pasta with spinach, tomatoes, walnuts, and pesto
9. Garnish with cheese
10. Serve and enjoy!

NUTRITION: *Calories: 361 Fat: 5 g Saturated Fat: 1 g Carbohydrates: 16 g Fiber: 4 g Sodium: 269 mg Protein: 33 g*

Prep & Cooking time: 30 minutes

Serving 8

Ingredients

- 1.3kg steak cubed
- 450ml bread crumbs Panko
- 5 ml dried mustard
- 150 ml flour
- 5 ml of pepper
- 7.5 ml salt
- 5 ml smoked paprika
- 250 ml milk
- 1 egg
- oil spray

Directions

1. Season the steak pieces with pepper and salt. In three separate bowls add the milk & egg, dry ingredients and in the third one add crumbs. First, dip in flour blend then egg mixture, and at the end in crumbs. Place these pieces in a foodi basket which has been sprayed with oil and preheated at 180 C.

2. Flip them after seven minutes and let them cook till they are browned to your preference.

Nutrition Values (Per Serving): Calories: Kcal 554 | Fat: 29g | Carbs: 28g | Protein: 43g

Preparation Time: 5-10 min.

Cooking Time: 95 min.

Servings: 8

INGREDIENTS:

- 450 ml chicken broth
- 6 anchovies fillets, chopped
- 10 ml olive oil
- 1.8kg bone-in lamb shoulder
- 1 rosemary sprig
- 5 ml dried oregano
- 5 ml garlic, minced
- Salt, to taste preference

DIRECTIONS:

1. Take Ninja Foodi multi-cooker, arrange it over a cooking platform, and open the top lid.

2. In the pot, add the oil; Select "Sear/Sauté" mode and select "Md: Hi" pressure level. Press "Stop/Start." After about 4-5 minutes, the oil will start simmering.

3. Add the lamb shoulder and stir-cook for about 2-3 minutes to brown evenly. Set aside.

4. In the pot, add the broth, anchovies, and garlic puree. Add the lamb shoulder on top and sprinkle with oregano, rosemary, and salt. Stir the mixture.

5. Secure the multi-cooker by locking it with the pressure lid; ensure to keep the pressure release valve locked/sealed.

6. Select "Pressure" mode and select the "Hi" pressure level. Then, set timer to 90 minutes and press "Stop/Start"; it will start the cooking process by building up inside pressure.

7. When the timer goes off, naturally release inside pressure for about 8-10 minutes. Then, quick-release pressure by adjusting the pressure valve to the Vent.

8. Open the lid, slice the lamb into small pieces, and serve warm.

Nutrition: Calories: 456 Fat: 19.5g Saturated Fat: 2g Trans Fat: 0g Carbohydrates: 3g Fiber: 0g Sodium: 958mg Protein: 48g

---

Preparation Time: 10 minutes

Cooking Time: 25 minutes

Servings: 4

INGREDIENTS:

- 1 yellow onion, chopped
- 30 ml rosemary, chopped
- 4 pork chops
- 450g gold potatoes halved
- 15 ml olive oil
- Pepper and salt to taste

DIRECTIONS:

1. Take your baking pan and grease with cooking spray, add ingredients and mix them
2. Pre-heat Ninja Foodi by pressing the "Roast" option and setting it to "185 degrees C" and timer to 25 minutes
3. Let it pre-heat until you hear a beep
4. Transfer baking dish to your Ninja Foodi Grill and let it bake until the timer runs out
5. Serve and enjoy once ready!

Nutrition: Calories: 186 Fat: 6 g Saturated Fat: 2 g Carbohydrates: 21 g Fiber: 3 g Sodium: 885 mg Protein: 10 g

---

Preparation Time: 10 minutes

Cooking Time: 10 minutes

Servings: 4

INGREDIENTS:

- 465g skirt steak
- Chimichurri Sauce
- 250 ml parsley, chopped
- 60 ml mint, chopped
- 30 ml oregano, chopped
- 3 garlic cloves, chopped
- 5 ml crushed red pepper
- 15 ml cumin, grounded
- 5 ml cayenne pepper
- 10 ml smoked paprika
- 5 ml salt
- 1.25 ml pepper
- 750 ml olive oil
- 45ml red wine vinegar

DIRECTIONS:

1. Get a bowl and mix all of the ingredients listed under Chimichurri section and mix them well
2. Cut the steak into 2 pieces of 225g portions
3. Take a resealable bag and add 60 ml of Chimichurri alongside the steak pieces and shake them to ensure that steak is coated well
4. Let it to chill in your fridge for 2-24 hours
5. Remove the steak from the fridge 30 minutes before cooking
6. Pre-heat Ninja Foodi by pressing the "Air Crisp" option and setting it to "195 Degrees C" and timer to 10 minutes

7. Transfer the steak to your Ninja Foodi Grill and cook for about 8-10 minutes if you are looking for a medium-rare finish

8. Garnish with 30 ml of Chimichurri sauce and enjoy!

NUTRITION: *Calories: 300 Fat: 18 g Saturated Fat: 4 g Carbohydrates: 80 g Fiber: 4 g Sodium: 415 mg Protein: 13 g*

Preparation Time: 10 minutes

Cooking Time: 15-20 minutes

Servings: 4

INGREDIENTS:

- 45ml sesame oil
- 45ml brown sugar
- 675g beef tips
- 4 garlic cloves, minced
- ½ apple, peeled and grated
- 75ml soy sauce
- 5 ml ground black pepper
- Salt and pepper to taste

DIRECTIONS:

1. Take your mixing bowl and add garlic, apple, sesame oil, sugar, soy sauce, pepper and salt
2. Add remaining ingredients and mix well
3. Add beef and coat for 1-2 hours, let it marinate
4. Pre-heat Ninja Foodi by pressing the GRILL" option and set it to "MED" and timer to 14 minutes
5. Let it pre-heat until you hear a beep
6. Arrange beef over grill grate, lock lid and cook for until timer reads 11 minutes
7. After that, cook until the internal temperature reaches 60 degrees C, cook for 3 minutes more if needed
8. Serve and enjoy!

Nutrition: Calories: 517 Fat: 29 g Saturated Fat: 5 g Carbohydrates: 16 g Fiber: 4 g Sodium: 1198 mg Protein: 36 g

Lamb and Garlic Sauce

Preparation Time: 10 minutes

Cooking Time: 5-10 minutes

Servings: 4

INGREDIENTS:

- 1 garlic bulb
- 45ml olive oil
- 15 ml fresh oregano, chopped
- Fresh ground black pepper
- 8 lamb chops

DIRECTIONS:

1. Pre-heat Ninja Foodi by pressing the "Air Crisp" option and setting it to "200 Degrees C" and timer to 10 minutes
2. Take the garlic bulb and drizzle with olive oil
3. Roast bulb for 12 minutes in Ninja Foodi Grill
4. Get a bowl and add in olive oil, salt, and pepper.
5. Coat lamb chops with 7.5 ml of herb/oil mix and marinate it for 5 minutes
6. Remove the garlic from cooking tray and add lamb to the Grill, cook for 5 minutes
7. Squeeze garlic clove with your hands over the herb oil mix, flavor with salt and pepper
8. Serve the lamb chops with garlic sauce
9. Enjoy!

Nutrition: Calories: 370 Fat: 35 g Saturated Fat: 6 g Carbohydrates: 1 g Fiber: 0.3 g Sodium: 160 mg Protein: 15 g

Prep & Cooking time: 35 minutes

Serving 8

Ingredients

- 4 boneless & skinless frozen chicken breasts (8–150 g/piece)
- 465g red salsa
- 1115g refried beans
- 15 ml kosher salt
- 30 ml taco seasoning
- 115g tortilla chips, in two parts
- 150 g cheese blend Mexican, in two parts

Toppings

- guacamole
- sour cream
- sliced fresh scallions

Directions

1. Cook salsa and frozen chicken at high pressure for 20 minutes. After it's done, shred the chicken in the pot. Put salt, taco seasoning, and beans.

2. Then place half of the tortillas over the chicken, then add cheese, and repeat. Air crisp for five minutes at 180 C when done, garnish with sour cream, guacamole, and scallions.

Nutrition Values (Per Serving)
Calories: Kcal 399 | Fat: 11g | Carbs: 13g | Protein: 59g

Prep & Cooking time: 50 minutes

Serving 2

Ingredients

- 30 ml olive oil

- 1 peeled & diced small onion

- 250 ml rice blend wild

- 15ml kosher salt

- 15 ml Moroccan seasoning

- 750 ml of chicken stock

- 2 chicken breasts frozen (8-280g/piece)

- 150 g trimmed green beans

- 5 ml black pepper

- 60 ml chopped fresh parsley

- 60 ml sauce honey mustard

Directions

1. Allow the foodi to preheat for about five minutes. Put onion and 15 ml oil. Sauté for three minutes then add Moroccan seasoning, 10 ml salt, and rice. Stir well to coat with oil then put chicken stock and mix. Put the chicken over the rack and carefully place it over the rice then cook for 22 minutes at high pressure.

2. In the meantime, mix the green beans with pepper, salt, and leftover oil.

3. When pressure cooking is done, take the rack out and mix in parsley and green beans.

4. Apply mustard honey sauce over the chicken and cook for the next ten minutes and it's ready to be served.

Nutrition Values (Per Serving)
Calories: Kcal 546 | Fat: 28g | Carbs: 42g | Protein: 31g

Preparation Time: 5-10 minutes

Cooking Time: 20 minutes

Servings: 5

INGREDIENTS:

- 4 boneless pork chops
- Salt and pepper
- 60 ml apple cider vinegar
- 60 ml of soy sauce
- 45ml Worcestershire sauce
- 450 ml ketchup
- 750 ml bourbon
- 250 ml packed brown sugar
- 7.5ml dry mustard powder

DIRECTIONS:

1. Set you Ninja Foodi to Grill mode and select Med, adjust the timer to 15 minutes
2. Let it preheat until you hear a beep
3. Arrange pork chops over grill grate, lock lid
4. Cook for 8 minutes, flip and cook for 2 minutes more If needed
5. Take a saucepan and heat remaining ingredients until the sauce boils
6. Lower the heat and simmer for 20 minutes
7. Serve pork chops with the sauce
8. *Enjoy!*

NUTRITION: *Calories: 346 Fat: 13 g Saturated Fat: 4 g Carbohydrates: 27 g Fiber: 0.4 g Sodium: 1324 mg Protein: 27 g*

Pressure Cooker Apricot Chicken

Prep & Cooking time: 20 minutes

 Serving 6

Ingredients

- 900g skinless, boneless chicken breasts, bite-sized
- 250 ml apricot jam
- 250 ml salad dressing Catalina
- 150 ml chicken broth
- 1 diced onion
- 30 g packet onion French soup mix
- 45ml of cornstarch

Directions

1. Other than cornstarch, put everything in the pot of foodi and cook for four minutes at high pressure. After that, switch to the sauté and in a bowl mix cornstarch with hot liquid and mix. Simmer for two minutes till it thickens and ready to be served.

Nutrition Values (Per Serving)
Calories-Kcal 566 | Fat: 30g | Carbs: 43g | Protein: 28g

Prep & Cooking time: 15 minutes

 Serving 6

Ingredients

- 10 frozen & packaged, chicken nuggets

Directions

1. Place the nuggets in the basket of foodi without overlapping them. Air crisp for about twelve minutes at 200 C. Flip them over after five minutes. Serve once done.

Nutrition Values (Per Serving)
Calories-Kcal 283 | Fat: 19g | Carbs: 6g | Protein: 21g

Preparation Time: 15 minutes

Cooking Time: 15 minutes

Servings: 4

INGREDIENTS:

- 4 cod fish fillets
- Salt and sugar to taste
- 5 ml sesame oil
- 250 ml water
- 75ml light soy sauce
- 5 ml dark soy sauce
- 45ml oil
- 5 slices ginger

DIRECTIONS:

1. Pat the cod fish fillets dry.
2. Season with the salt, sugar and sesame oil. Marinate for 15 minutes.
3. Set the Ninja Foodi to air crisp.
4. Put the fish on top of the basket. Cook at 175 degrees C for 3 minutes.
5. Flip and cook for 2 minutes. Take the fish out and set aside.
6. Put remaining ingredients in the pot.
7. Set it to sauté. Simmer and pour over the fish before serving.

NUTRITION: *Calories 303 Total Fat 13.1g Saturated Fat 1.9g Cholesterol 99mg Sodium 144mg Total Carbohydrate 2.9g Dietary Fiber 0.5g Total Sugars 0.1g Protein 41.5g Potassium 494mg*

Prep & Cooking time: 27 minutes

Serving 4

Ingredients

- 10 medium-size chicken legs
- 125 ml bbq sauce
- 250 ml water

Directions

1. Cover the chicken with half of the bbq sauce and put it in the foodi basket. Add 250 ml of water to the base and place the basket in it. Now pressure cook at high for about 12 minutes. Now take out the chicken and again spray the basket with oil.

2. Brush the chicken with the second half of the bbq sauce and cook for ten minutes at 200 C in the air crisp mode.

Nutrition Values (Per Serving)
Calories: Kcal 451 | Fat: 52g | Carbs: 15g | Protein: 53g

Prep & Cooking time: 55 minutes

Serving 6

Ingredients

- 1 (1.8kg) defrosted turkey breast
- 1 onion
- 2 large red or russet potatoes
- 375 ml chicken broth
- 2.5 ml thyme
- 2.5 ml oregano
- 2.5 ml powdered garlic
- 2.5 ml powdered onion
- 1.25 ml salt
- 0.5ml of pepper
- 45ml of olive oil
- 5 ml of garlic salt

Directions

1. Make a trivet with the halved potatoes and place turkey over it. Put onions around it and add all of the seasonings and herbs. Pour broth around the meat.

2. Cook at high pressure for thirty minutes.

3. If you like the turkey crispy then take out all the other ingredients, sprinkle the garlic salt and oil then let the turkey air crisp for ten minutes at 195 C. then it's ready to be served.

Nutrition Values (Per Serving)
Calories-Kcal 246 | Fat: 9g | Carbs: 11g | Protein: 30g

Prep & Cooking time: 37 minutes

Serving 6

Ingredients

- 3 skinless boneless chicken breasts, pounded flat
- 6 jalapenos
- 750 ml softened cream cheese
- 125 ml Monterey jack
- 5 ml of cumin
- 9 bacon strips
- salt & pepper

Directions

1. Cut the chicken pieces in half and pound it to 1/8 inch thickness and season with pepper and salt. In a separate bowl mix both the cheese with cumin.

2. Deseed the jalapenos after slicing them in half then fill with the cheese mixture. Now fold the stuffed jalapenos in chicken. In the end, wrap with bacon and lock with the toothpick.

3. Cook for twenty minutes at 170 C and flip them midway. Once done, let them cool for five minutes then serve.

Nutrition Values (Per Serving)
Calories: Kcal 407 | Fat: 29g | Carbs: 3g | Protein: 32g

Prep & Cooking time: 50 minutes

 Serving 4

Ingredients

- 60 ml of olive oil
- 5 ml sea salt fine grind
- 2.5 ml of pepper
- 150 g red potatoes
- 2 zucchinis medium
- 1 yellow squash medium
- 1 red onion
- 1 garlic bulb
- 465g chicken breast
- 8 rosemary sprigs fresh
- 2 lemons

Directions

1. Cut potatoes in ¼ths and toss them in 15 ml olive oil then a mixture of pepper and salt. Air roast them for about 10 minutes at 450 F on the tray of foodi.

2. Meanwhile, chop the zucchini and squash in a similar size to that of potatoes. Crush the garlic and thinly slice the onion (save the ¼ of the onion for chicken). Pour 15 ml olive oil and pepper salt mixture. Mix well the veggies. Keep aside the ¼" sliced lemons.

3. Now rub the chicken with pepper salt mixture and oil.

4. Once the potatoes are done, flip them over.

5. Make three parts in the pan. One for the potatoes, chicken, and veggies each. Place rosemary sprigs over the veggies and potatoes section. For chicken, place the leftover onions, rosemary sprigs, and lemon slices in the base and place chicken over it, and above the

chicken add rosemary sprigs. Add the leftover oil and pepper salt mixture.

6. Bake for about thirty minutes. When the chicken is cooked, take it out and broil the remaining veggies for ten minutes. Enjoy.

Nutrition Values (Per Serving)
Calories: Kcal 345 | Fat: 17g | Carbs: 21g | Protein: 28g

Preparation Time: 10 minutes

Cooking Time: 20 minutes

Servings: 4

INGREDIENTS:

- 1 ripe mango
- 7.5 ml red chili paste
- 45ml fresh coriander
- 1 lime juice
- 450g fish fillet
- 50g shredded coconut

DIRECTIONS:

1. Pre-heat Ninja Foodi by pressing the "AIR CRISP" option and setting it to "177 Degrees C" and timer to 20 minutes
2. let it pre-heat until you hear a beep
3. Peel the mango and cut it up into small cubes
4. Mix the mango cubes in a bowl alongside 2.5 ml of red chili paste, juice, zest of lime and 15 ml of coriander
5. Puree the fish fillet in a food processor and mix with 5 ml of salt and 1 egg
6. Add the rest of the lime zest, lime juice, and red chili paste
7. Mix well alongside the remaining coriander
8. Add 30 ml of coconut and green onion
9. Put the rest of the coconut on a soup plate
10. Divide the fish mix into 12 portions and shape them into cakes
11. Coat with coconut
12. Transfer six pieces of cakes to your Ninja Foodi Grill, cook for 8 minutes until golden brown
13. Repeat until all batter used up, serve with mango salsa and enjoy!

NUTRITION: *Calories: 150 Fat: 8 g Saturated Fat: 4 g Carbohydrates: 15 g Fiber: 2 g Sodium: 1236 mg Protein: 10 g*

Prep & Cooking time: 26 minutes

 Serving 6

Ingredients

- 7.5ml of cayenne pepper
- 15 ml of paprika
- 15 ml powdered chili
- 30 ml powdered garlic
- 7.5ml of pepper
- 30 ml of salt
- 750 ml brown sugar
- 16 of chicken wings
- 15 ml of garlic salt
- oil spray
- 5 ml of cinnamon

Directions

1. Combine all the ingredients to make rub except for the wings.

2. Wash the wings and dry them then pour some olive oil. Add half of the dry rub in the freezer bag then put six wings and coat well. Spray the foodi container with oil and place wings in it without overlapping them. At 200 C cook for 15 minutes and don't forget to flip them midway.

3. Repeat the same process with the next batches.

Nutrition Values (Per Serving)
Calories: Kcal 409 | Fat: 21g | Carbs: 31g | Protein: 25g

Serves 4

Prep Time

30 Minutes

Ingredients:

- 45ml olive oil

- 1 small onion, chopped (about 150 ml)

- 2 large garlic cloves, minced

- 1 jalapeño pepper, seeded and chopped (about 30 ml)

- 250 ml long-grain white rice, thoroughly rinsed

- 75 ml red salsa

- 60 ml tomato sauce

- 125 ml **Roasted Vegetable Stock**, low-sodium vegetable broth, or water

- 5 ml **Mexican/Southwestern Seasoning Mix**, or store-bought mix

- 1 (465g) can pinto beans, drained and rinsed

- 5 ml kosher salt (or 2.5 ml fine salt)

- 15 ml chopped fresh cilantro (optional)

Direction:

1. On your Foodi™, select Sear/Sauté and adjust to Medium to preheat the inner pot. Press Start. Allow the pot to preheat for 5 minutes. Pour in the olive oil and heat until shimmering. Add the onion, garlic, and jalapeño. Cook for 2 minutes, stirring occasionally, or until fragrant and beginning to soften. Stir in the rice, salsa, tomato sauce, vegetable stock, seasoning, pinto beans, and salt. (If using water, add another 2.5 ml of kosher salt or 1.25 ml of fine salt).

2. Lock the Pressure Lid into place, making sure the valve is set to Seal. Select Pressure and adjust the pressure to High and the cook time to 6 minutes. Press Start.

3. After cooking, let the pressure release naturally for 10 minutes, then quick release any remaining pressure. Carefully unlock and remove the Pressure Lid. Stir in the cilantro (if using) and serve.

Per Serving *Calories: 384; Total fat: 12g; Saturated fat: 2g; Cholesterol: 0mg; Sodium: 1089mg; Carbohydrates: 60g; Fiber: 7g; Protein: 10g*

Prep & Cooking time: 20 minutes

Serving 2

Ingredients

- 2 boneless, skinless & large frozen chicken breasts
- 2.5 ml of salt
- 1.25 ml pepper
- 1.25 ml powdered garlic
- 1.25 ml flaked parsley

Directions

1. Place the frozen chicken pieces in a foodi container and scatter the rest of the dry ingredients uniformly over the chicken.

2. Cook for fifteen minutes at 180 C then make sure it's done before slicing. Let it stay for five minutes and then serve.

Nutrition Values (Per Serving)
Calories: Kcal 260 | Fat: 6g | Carbs: 1g | Protein: 48g

Serves 4

Prep Time

40 Minutes

Ingredients:

- 1 large eggplant, cut into ¾-inch-thick rounds
- 10 ml kosher salt (or 5 ml fine salt)
- 45ml melted unsalted butter
- 375 ml panko bread crumbs
- 75 ml grated Parmesan or similar cheese
- 450 ml Marinara Sauce
- 250 ml shredded mozzarella cheese

Direction:

1. Sprinkle the eggplant slices on both sides with the salt and place on a wire rack over a rimmed baking sheet to drain for 5 to 10 minutes.

2. While the eggplant drains, in a medium bowl, stir together the melted butter, panko, and Parmesan cheese. Set aside.

3. Rinse the eggplant slices and blot them dry. Place them in a single layer (as much as possible) in the Foodi's inner pot and cover with the marinara sauce.

4. Lock the Pressure Lid into place, making sure the valve is set to Seal. Select Pressure and adjust the pressure to High and the cook time to 5 minutes. Press Start.

5. After cooking, use a quick pressure release. Carefully unlock and remove the Pressure Lid.

6. Cover the eggplant slices with the mozzarella cheese.

7. Close the Crisping Lid. Select Bake/Roast and adjust the temperature to 190°C and the cook time to 2 minutes. Press Start.

8. When cooking is complete, open the lid and sprinkle the eggplant and cheese with the panko mixture. Close the Crisping Lid again. Select

Bake/Roast and adjust the temperature to 190°C and the cook time to 8 minutes. Press Start. When done, the topping should be brown and crisp; if not, broil for 1 to 2 minutes more. Serve immediately.

Per Serving *Calories: 434; Total fat: 20g; Saturated fat: 11g; Cholesterol: 52mg; Sodium: 906mg; Carbohydrates: 47g; Fiber: 8g; Protein: 18g*

Preparation Time: 10 minutes

Cooking Time: 10 minutes

Servings: 4

INGREDIENTS:

- 450g shrimp, peeled and deveined
- 2 eggs
- 125 ml bread crumbs
- 125 ml onion, diced
- 5 ml ginger
- 5 ml garlic powder
- Salt and pepper to taste

DIRECTIONS:

1. In one bowl, beat the two eggs. In a new bowl, put the rest of the ingredients.
2. Dip the shrimp first in the eggs and then in the spice mixture.
3. Place in the Ninja Foodi basket. Seal the crisping lid. Choose air crisp function.
4. Cook at 175 degrees C for 10 minutes.

NUTRITION: *Calories 229 Total Fat 4.9g Saturated Fat 1.4g Cholesterol 321mg Sodium 407mg Total Carbohydrate 13.8g Dietary Fiber 1.1g Total Sugars 1.8g Protein 30.7g Potassium 283mg*

Preparation Time: 10 minutes

Cooking Time: 10 minutes

Servings: 4

INGREDIENTS:

- 10 ml peppercorns
- 5 ml salt
- 5 ml sugar
- 450g shrimp
- 45ml rice flour
- 30 ml oil

DIRECTIONS:

1. Set the Ninja Foodi to sauté. Roast the peppercorns for 1 minute. Let them cool.
2. Crush the peppercorns and add the salt and sugar.
3. Coat the shrimp with this mixture and then with flour.
4. Sprinkle oil on the Ninja Foodi basket. Place the shrimp on top.
5. Cook at 175 degrees C for 10 minutes, flipping halfway through.

NUTRITION: Calories 228 Total Fat 8.9g Saturated Fat 1.5g Cholesterol 239mg Sodium 859mg Total Carbohydrate 9.3g Dietary Fiber 0.5g Total Sugars 1g Protein 26.4g Potassium 211mg

---

Preparation Time: 15 minutes

Cooking Time: 15 minutes

Servings: 2

INGREDIENTS:

- 2 cans tuna flakes
- 7.5 ml almond flour
- 5 ml dried dill
- 15 ml mayo
- 2.5ml onion powder
- 5 ml garlic powder
- Salt and pepper to taste
- 15 ml lemon juice

DIRECTIONS:

1. Mix all the ingredients in a bowl. Form patties. Set the tuna patties on the Ninja Foodi basket. Seal the crisping lid. Set it to air crisp.
2. Cook at 200 degrees C for 10 minutes. Flip and cook for 5 more minutes.

NUTRITION: *Calories 141 Total Fat 6.4g Saturated Fat 0.7g Cholesterol 17mg Sodium 148mg Total Carbohydrate 5.2g Dietary Fiber 1g Total Sugars 1.2g Protein 17g Potassium 48mg*

Lemon Garlic Shrimp

Preparation Time: 15 minutes

Cooking Time: 25 minutes

Servings: 4

INGREDIENTS:

- 450g shrimp, peeled and deveined
- 15 ml olive oil
- 4 cloves garlic, minced
- 15 ml lemon juice
- Salt to taste

DIRECTIONS:

1. Mix the olive oil, salt, lemon juice and garlic. Toss shrimp in the mixture.
2. Marinate for 15 minutes. Place the shrimp in the Ninja Foodi basket.
3. Seal the crisping lid. Select the air crisp setting.
4. Cook at 175 degrees C for 8 minutes. Flip and cook for 2 more minutes.

NUTRITION: Calories 170 Total Fat 5.5g Saturated Fat 1.1g Cholesterol 239mg Sodium 317mg Total Carbohydrate 2.8g Dietary Fiber 0.1g Total Sugars 0.1g Protein 26.1g Potassium 209mg

---

Crispy Fish Nuggets

Preparation Time: 15 minutes

Cooking Time: 15 minutes

Servings: 4

INGREDIENTS:

- 450g cod fillet, sliced into 8 pieces
- Salt and pepper to taste
- 125 ml flour
- 15 ml egg with 5 ml water
- 250 ml bread crumbs
- 15 ml vegetable oil

DIRECTIONS:

1. Season the fish with salt and pepper. Cover with the flour.
2. Dunk the fish in the egg wash and into the bread crumbs.
3. Place the fish nuggets in the Ninja Foodi basket. Set it to air crisp function.
4. Seal with the crisping lid. Cook at 1800 degrees C for 15 minutes.

NUTRITION: *Calories 234 Total Fat 5.4g Saturated Fat 1g Cholesterol 25mg Sodium 229mg Total Carbohydrate 31.4g Dietary Fiber 1.7g Total Sugars 1.7g Protein 14.1g Potassium 70mg*

Preparation Time: 5-10 minutes

Cooking Time: 13 minutes

Servings: 3

INGREDIENTS:

- 1.25 ml salt
- 750 ml breadcrumbs
- 60 ml parmesan cheese, grated
- 1.25 ml ground dried thyme
- 60 ml butter, melted
- 450g haddock fillets
- 750 ml milk

DIRECTIONS:

1. Coat fish fillets in milk, season with salt and keep it on the side
2. Take a mixing bowl and add breadcrumbs, parmesan, cheese, thyme and combine well
3. Coat fillets in bread crumb mixture
4. Pre-heat Ninja Foodi by pressing the "BAKE" option and setting it to "162 Degrees C" and timer to 13 minutes
5. Let it pre-heat until you hear a beep
6. Arrange fish fillets directly over Grill Grate, lock lid and cook for 8 minutes, flip and cook for the remaining time
7. Serve and enjoy!

NUTRITION: Calories: 450 Fat: 27 g Saturated Fat: 12 g Carbohydrates: 16 g Fiber: 3 g Sodium: 1056 mg Protein: 44 g

Prep Time: 15 mins.

Cooking Time: 6 hours

Number of Servings: 8

Ingredients:

- 450g. potatoes
- 450g Sweet potatoes
- 6ml salt
- 15 ml + 5 ml olive oil
- 1 2.5 ml garlic powder
- 5 ml pepper
- 2 150 ml Emmental cheese, grated
- 75ml chives, chopped

Directions:

1. Place the pot in your Ninja Foodi according to your manual.
2. Place the Pressure Lid on your Ninja Foodi according to your manual and ensure the pressure valve is at the VENT position.
3. Wash the potatoes thoroughly if not peeling them.
4. Mix all of your ingredients, saving the cheese and the chives aside.
5. Cover with the lid and press "Function". Use the dial to select the "SLOW COOK" function.
6. Press "Temp" and use the dial to set the temperature to LOW
7. Press "Time" and use the dial to set the timer to 6 hours.
8. Press the "START/STOP" button to start the cooking.
9. When done, remove from the heat and top with the cheese and the chives.
10. Serve hot.

Nutritional Values (Per Serving): Calories: 220 Fat: 14g Saturated Fat: 3g Trans Fat: 0g
Carbohydrates: 12g Fiber: 2g Sodium: 642mg Protein: 12g

Prep & Cooking time: 31 minutes

 Serving 6

Ingredients

- 2 skinless & boneless chicken breasts, 2" pieces
- 1 zucchini (1" slices)
- 1 onion (1" slices)
- ½ pint of grape tomatoes
- 15 ml minced garlic
- 30 ml wine vinegar
- 1 juiced lemon
- 5 ml of oregano
- 60 ml olive oil
- salt & pepper as per taste

Directions

1. Coat the chicken pieces with a mixture of lemon juice, vinegar, garlic, olive oil, and oregano. Let it stay for 20 minutes in the refrigerator.

2. Toss all the chopped veggies with olive oil and season with pepper and salt.

3. Prepare the skewers as per the size of the foodi container. Then alternatively with the chicken add onion, zucchini, and tomato pieces. Cook them at 193 Cfor 15 minutes flipping them midway and then serve.

Nutrition Values (Per Serving)
Calories: Kcal 194 | Fat: 11g | Carbs: 7g | Protein: 17g

Serves 4

45 Minutes

Ingredients:

- 4 small russet potatoes, scrubbed clean
- 60 ml heavy (whipping) cream
- 60 ml sour cream
- 125 ml chopped roasted red pepper
- 5 ml Cajun Seasoning Mix or a store-bought mix
- 375 ml shredded white Cheddar cheese
- 4 scallions, white and green parts, chopped, divided
- 75 ml grated Parmesan or similar cheese

Direction:

1. Pour 250 ml of water into the Foodi's™ inner pot. Place the Reversible Rack in the pot in the lower position and place the potatoes on top.

2. Lock the Pressure Lid into place, making sure the valve is set to Seal. Select Pressure and adjust the pressure to High and the cook time to 10 minutes. Press Start.

3. After cooking, let the pressure release naturally for 5 minutes, then quick release any remaining pressure. Carefully unlock and remove the Pressure Lid.

4. Using tongs, transfer the potatoes to a cutting board. When cool enough to handle, slice off a ½-inch strip from the top, long side of each potato. Scoop the flesh into a large bowl, including the flesh from the tops. Add the heavy cream and sour cream. Using a potato masher, mash until fairly smooth. Stir in the roasted red pepper, seasoning, and Cheddar cheese. Set aside about 30 ml of the green part of the scallions, and stir the rest into the potatoes. Spoon the mashed potato mixture into the potato skins, mounding it slightly. Sprinkle the Parmesan evenly over the tops.

5. Empty the water out of the inner pot and return it to the base.

6. Place the Cook & Crisp™ Basket into the pot. Close the Crisping Lid. Select Air Crisp and adjust the temperature to 375°F and the time to 2 minutes to preheat. Press Start.

7. When the Foodi™ is heated, open the lid and place the potatoes in the basket. Close the Crisping Lid. Select Air Crisp and adjust the temperature to 190°C and the cook time to 15 minutes. Press Start.

8. When done, the potatoes should be lightly browned and crisp on top. Let cool for a few minutes and serve garnished with the reserved scallions.

Per Serving *Calories: 429; Total fat: 25g; Saturated fat: 15g; Cholesterol: 80mg; Sodium: 418mg; Carbohydrates: 35g; Fiber: 3g; Protein: 18g*

Prep & Cooking time: 25 minutes

Serving 6

Ingredients

- 900g skinless boneless & trimmed chicken thighs (bite-size chunks)
- 750 ml teriyaki sauce
- ¼ diced onion

Directions

1. Coat the chicken and onion well with the teriyaki sauce and let it stay for an hour. Put the chicken in a preheated foodi at 193 C.

2. Let it cook for eight minutes tossing them after four minutes. Check if it's done then serve with rice.

Nutrition Values (Per Serving)
Calories: Kcal 282 | Fat: 19g | Carbs: 6g | Protein: 21g

Prep Time: 10 mins.

Cooking Time: 20 mins.

Number of Servings: 8

Ingredients:

- 900gs. potatoes, peeled and diced
- 2 thick slices of bacon, thickly chopped
- 10 marjoram leaves
- 75ml milk
- 30 ml butter
- 15 ml white rum
- 5 ml salt
- 1.25ml pepper

Directions:

1. Place the cooking pot in your Ninja Foodi according to your manual.
2. Press "Function" and turn the dial to the "Sear/Sauté" function.
3. Press "Temp" and use the dial to adjust the temperature to Medium-High.
4. Press the "START/STOP" button to start cooking.
5. Place the bacon in the pot and cook until the bacon is crispy.
6. Empty the bacon on a dish lined with a paper towel.
7. Put the marjoram in the pot and cook until crispy. When done empty on the dish with the bacon.
8. Add the potatoes to the pot and fill with water making sure it doesn't exceed the max line.
9. Close the lid and check that the pressure valve is set to sealed.
10. Press "Function" and turn the dial to the "PRESSURE COOK" function.

11. Press "Temp" and use the dial to adjust the temperature to High.

12. Press "Time" and use the dial to adjust the temperature to 13 minutes

13. Press the "START/STOP" button to start cooking.

14. When it's finished, perform a Natural release for 10 minutes.

15. Set the pressure valve to vent to release the rest of the pressure before opening the lid.

16. Empty the potatoes into a bowl and use an immersion blender or a fork to mash them.

17. Add the bacon, the rum, the milk, the butter, and season with salt and pepper to your liking.

18. Mix well to combine.

19. Serve hot topped with the crispy marjoram

Nutritional Values (Per Serving): *Calories: 161 Fat: 2.4g   Saturated Fat: 2.4g Trans Fat: 0.1g Carbohydrates: 26g   Fiber: 3g   Sodium: 374mg Protein: 4g*

Prep & Cooking time: 30 minutes

Serving 8

Ingredients

- 900g chicken legs
- 250 ml buttermilk
- 250 ml bread crumbs
- 250 ml white flour
- 2.5 ml of baking powder
- 2.5 ml salt
- 2.5 ml pepper
- 2.5 ml powdered garlic
- 2.5 ml powdered onion
- 2.5 ml paprika
- 2.5 ml oregano
- 1 stick melted butter

Directions

1. Soak chicken in buttermilk overnight or a minimum of two hours in a freezer bag.

2. Now preheat the foodi at 195 C.

3. Combine flour, breadcrumbs, baking powder, and all the dry seasonings in a bowl. Now coat the chicken pieces one at a time in the crumbs mixture.

4. Spray some oil in the foodi container and place the chicken pieces in it, avoiding overlapping them. Cook for fifteen minutes at 195 C. Now brush them with butter after taking them out then put back once again and cook for additional ten minutes over the other side.

5. If needed, put the second batch and cook as described earlier.

Nutrition Values (Per Serving)

Calories: Kcal 347 | Fat: 23g | Carbs: 20g | Protein: 14g

Prep & Cooking time: 25 minutes

Serving 4

Ingredients

- 3 skinless & boneless chicken breasts
- 125 ml water
- 750 ml bbq sauce
- 5 ml powdered garlic
- 2.5 ml salt

Directions

1. Mix garlic powder, salt, and bbq sauce in a small bowl. Take out half of the bbq mixture in another bowl and mix with water. Pour it in the base of the pot. Then place the trivet in it and arrange the chicken breasts over it and apply the remaining sauce.

2. Now cook at high for six minutes. Take the chicken out and discard the liquid. Then serve the chicken.

Nutrition Values (Per Serving)
Calories: Kcal 288 | Fat: 5g | Carbs: 22g | Protein: 37g

Prep Time: 5 mins.

Cooking Time: 4 hours.

Servings: 16

Ingredients:

- 600g fresh corn kernels, drained and rinsed if canned
- 325ml milk
- 20ml sugar
- 1.5ml pepper
- 280g. cream cheese
- 1 1/3 sticks butter, cubed

Directions:

1. Place the pot in your Ninja Foodi according to your manual.
2. Place the Pressure Lid on your Ninja Foodi according to your manual and ensure the pressure valve is at the VENT position.
3. Put the corn in the pot and stir in the milk, pepper, and the sugar.
4. Add the butter and the cream cheese. Don't stir.
5. Cover with the lid.
6. Press "Function" and use the dial to select the "SLOW COOK" function.
7. Press "Temp" and use the dial to set the temperature to HIGH
8. Press "Time" and use the dial to set the timer to 4 hours.
9. Press the "START/STOP" button to start the cooking.
10. When done, remove from the heat and stir well.
11. Serve warm with barbecued meats.

Nutritional Values (Per Serving): *Calories: 166 Fat: 13.5g Saturated Fat: 8.4g Trans Fat: 0.3g Carbohydrates: 10g Fiber: 1g Sodium: 148mg Protein: 3g*

Prep & Cooking time: 40 minutes

Serving 6

Ingredients

- 1 halved lengthwise large zucchini in 1" chunks
- 6 chicken thighs boneless, skinless, cut into bite-size pieces
- 1 red or yellow onion, chopped in large pieces
- 375 ml grape tomatoes
- 1 minced garlic clove
- 1 juiced lemon
- 60 ml olive oil
- 30 ml wine vinegar
- 5 ml of oregano
- oil spray

Directions

1. Mix lemon juice, olive oil, oregano, vinegar, and garlic and add in the chicken pieces and coat them well. Then refrigerate for thirty minutes.

2. Now add the chicken and veggies to the wooden skewers. Then place them in foodi and cook them for 16 minutes approx. at 193 C.

Nutrition Values (Per Serving)
Calories: Kcal 211 | Fat: 14g | Carbs: 6g | Protein: 17g

Prep & Cooking time: 60 minutes

Serving 10

Ingredients

- 675g skinless, boneless chicken breasts
- 1 diced onion
- 2 peeled carrots, cut in dials
- 2 sliced celery stalks
- 250 ml frozen peas
- 30 ml garlic minced
- 2.5 ml thyme
- 2.5 ml pepper
- 2.5 ml salt
- 250 ml chicken broth
- 60 ml white flour
- 375 ml milk
- 1 biscuit roll refrigerated

Directions

1. Put the first ten ingredients in a foodi and cook for twelve minutes at high pressure. Take out the chicken and cut it in cubes. Now let the other ingredients boil at a sauté setting and add flour.

2. Once it starts to thicken, add chicken and milk. Let it cook for five minutes.

3. Place the biscuits over the chicken filling. Air crisp for eight minutes at 180 C flipping them midway. Let it cool for ten minutes before serving.

Nutrition Values (Per Serving)
Calories: Kcal 367 | Fat: 19g | Carbs: 29g | Protein: 19g

Serves 4

Prep Time

30 Minutes, Plus Soaking Time

Ingredients:

- 15 ml plus 5 ml kosher salt (or 10 ml fine salt), divided
- 395g dried cannellini beans
- 60ml plus 5 ml extra-virgin olive oil, divided
- 1 quart water
- 45ml freshly squeezed lemon juice
- 5 ml ground cumin
- 1.25 ml freshly ground black pepper
- 1 medium red or green bell pepper, chopped (about 250 ml)
- 1 large celery stalk, chopped (about 125 ml)
- 3 or 4 scallions, chopped (about 75 ml)
- 1 large tomato, seeded and chopped (about 125 ml)
- ½ cucumber, peeled, seeded, and chopped (about 750 ml)
- 250 ml crumbled feta cheese (optional)
- 30 ml minced fresh mint
- 60 ml minced fresh parsley

Direction:

1. In a large bowl, dissolve 15 ml of kosher salt (or 12.5 mls of fine salt) in 1 quart of water. Add the beans and soak at room temperature for 8 to 24 hours.

2. Drain and rinse the beans. Place them in the Foodi's™ inner pot. Add 5 ml of olive oil and stir to coat the beans. Add the 1 quart of water and 2.5 ml of kosher salt (or 1.25 ml of fine salt).

3. Lock the Pressure Lid into place, making sure the valve is set to Seal. Select Pressure and adjust the pressure to High and the cook time to 5 minutes. Press Start.

4. While the beans cook and the pressure releases, in a small jar with a tight-fitting lid, combine the lemon juice and 45ml of olive oil. Add the cumin, the remaining 2.5 ml of kosher salt (or 1.25 ml of fine salt), and the pepper. Cover the jar and shake the dressing until thoroughly combined. (Alternatively, whisk the dressing in a small bowl, but it's easier to make it in a jar.)

5. After cooking, let the pressure release naturally for 10 minutes, then quick release any remaining pressure. Carefully unlock and remove the Pressure Lid.

6. Drain the beans and pour them into a bowl. Immediately pour the dressing over the beans and toss to coat. Let cool to room temperature, stirring occasionally.

7. Add the bell pepper, celery, scallions, tomato, cucumber, and feta cheese (if using; omit for a dairy-free and vegan dish) to the beans. Toss gently. Right before serving, add the mint and parsley and toss to combine.

Per Serving *Calories: 489; Total fat: 16g; Saturated fat: 2g; Cholesterol: 0mg; Sodium: 622mg; Carbohydrates: 66g; Fiber: 27g; Protein: 25g*

Dessert Recipes

Ultimate Cheese Dredged Cauliflower Snack

(Prepping time: 10 minutes\ Cooking time: 30 minutes |For 4 servings)

Ingredients

- 15 ml mustard
- 1 head cauliflower
- 5 ml avocado mayonnaise
- 125 ml parmesan cheese, grated
- 60 ml butter, cut into small pieces

Directions

1. Set your Ninja Foodi to Saute mode and add butter and cauliflower
2. Saute for 3 minutes. Add remaining ingredients and stir
3. Lock lid and cook on HIGH pressure for 30 minutes. Release pressure naturally over 10 minutes
4. Serve and enjoy!

Nutrition Values (Per Serving) *Calories: 155 Fat: 13g Carbohydrates: 4g Protein: 6g*

Grape Jelly

Prep Time: 10 mins.

Cooking Time: 20 mins.

Number of Servings: 5 quarts

Ingredients:

- 1800 grams Concord grapes
- 1350 grams seedless grapes
- 125ml water
- 340 grams liquid pectin
- 3.5 litre sugar

Directions:

1. Wash and sort the grapes thoroughly. Discard the stems.
2. Add grapes in the pot and use the immersion blender to crush them.
3. Add the water.
4. Press "Function" and turn the dial to the "PRESSURE COOK" function.
5. Press "Temp" and use the dial to adjust the temperature to High.
6. Press "Time" and use the dial to adjust the temperature to 3 minutes
7. Press "Start/Stop" to start cooking.
8. When done, perform a natural release of 15 minutes.
9. When the pressure releases open the lid and use a fine mesh sieve lined with a damp cheesecloth to strain the juice.
10. Return juice to the pot and add the sugar.
11. Press "Function" and turn the dial to the "Sear/Sauté" function.
12. Press "Temp" and use the dial to adjust the temperature to High.
13. Press the "START/STOP" button to start cooking.
14. Bring to a boil then add in the pectin. Boil for 1 minute.
15. Turn off the heat and skim off the foam.

16. Empty into hot, sterilized air-tight glass jars.

17. Fill about to 1" lower than the lid.

18. Seal and allow to cool for 24 hours.

19. Keep in the refrigerator for up to 5 weeks or the freezer for up to 8 months.

Nutritional Values (Per 15ml): *Calories: 23 Fat: 0g Saturated Fat: 0g Trans Fat: 0g Carbohydrates: 6g Fiber: 0g Sodium: 0mg Protein: 0g*

The Onion and Smoky Mushroom Medley

(Prepping time: 5 minutes\ Cooking time: 2 minutes |For 4 servings)

Ingredients

- 15 ml ghee
- 1 carton (225g) button mushrooms, sliced
- 1 onion, diced
- 2.5 ml salt
- 30 ml coconut aminos
- 0.5ml smoked paprika

Directions

1. Set your Ninja Foodi to Saute mode and add ghee, let it heat up
2. Add mushrooms, onion and seasoning, Saute for 5 minutes
3. Lock lid and cook on HIGH pressure for 3 minutes
4. Quick release pressure
5. Serve warm and enjoy!

Nutrition Values (Per Serving) Calories: 268 Fat: 20g Carbohydrates: 11g Protein: 10g

---

Cool Beet Chips

(Prepping time: 10 minutes\ Cooking time: 8 hours |For 8 servings)

Ingredients

- ½ beet, peeled and cut into 1/8-inch slices

Directions

1. Arrange beet slices in single layer in the Cook and Crisp basket

2. Place the basket in the pot and close the crisping lid

3. Press the Dehydrate button and let it dehydrate for 8 hours at 57 degrees C

4. Once the dehydrating is done, remove the basket from pot and transfer slices to your Air Tight container, serve and enjoy!

Nutrition Values (Per Serving) Calories: 35 Fat: 0g Carbohydrates: 8g Protein: 1g

Lovely Cauliflower Soup

(Prepping time: 10 minutes\ Cooking time:301 minutes |For 5 servings)

Ingredients

- 5 slices bacon, chopped
- 1 onion, chopped
- 3 garlic cloves, minced
- 1 cauliflower head, trimmed
- 1 litre chicken broth
- 250 ml almond milk
- 5 ml salt
- 5 ml black pepper
- 375 ml cheddar cheese, shredded
- Sour cream and chopped fresh chives for serving

Directions

1. Set your pot to Saute mode and pre-heat it for 5 minutes on HIGH settings
2. Add bacon, onion, garlic to your pot and cook for 5 minutes
3. Reserve bacon for garnish
4. Add cauliflower, chicken broth to the pot and place pressure cooker lid, seal the pressure valves
5. Cook on HIGH pressure for 10 minutes, quick release the pressure once did
6. Add milk, and mash the soup reaches your desired consistency
7. Season with salt, pepper and sprinkle cheese evenly on top of the soup
8. Close crisping lid and Broil for 5 minutes
9. Once done, top with reserved crispy bacon and serve with sour cream and chives
10. Enjoy!

__Nutrition Values (Per Serving)__ Calories: 253 Fat: 17g Carbohydrates: 12g Protein: 13g

Prep Time: 10 mins.

Cooking Time: 11 mins.

Servings: 8

Ingredients:

- 4 Apples, cored and cut into wedges
- 1 75ml flour
- 4 eggs, whisked
- 1 75ml graham crackers in crumbs
- 125 ml brown sugar
- 15 ml cinnamon

Directions:

1. Place the crisper basket in your Ninja Foodi according to your manual. Grease thoroughly.
2. Place the flour in a bowl. The egg in another bowl, and the sugar, cinnamon, and cracker crumbs in a third bowl.
3. Dip the fruit in each bowl in the order above, making sure they're well coated.
4. Place the fruit in the crisper basket.
5. Press "Function" then turn the dial to "AIR CRISP".
6. Press "Temp" then turn the dial to 193 C.
7. Press "Time" then turn the dial to 11 minutes.
8. Close the lid and press the "START/STOP" button. The unit will preheat automatically.
9. Cook, turning the food around halfway through the cooking process.
10. Serve immediately!

Nutritional Values (Per Serving): *Calories: 110 Fat: 4g   Saturated Fat: 2.1g Trans Fat: 0.1g Carbohydrates: 19g   Fiber: 2g   Sodium: 48mg   Protein: 1g*

Elegant Broccoli Pops

(Prepping time: 60 minutes\ Cooking time: 12 minutes |For 4 servings)

Ingredients

- 75ml parmesan cheese, grated
- 450 ml cheddar cheese, grated
- Salt and pepper to taste
- 3 eggs, beaten
- 750 ml broccoli florets
- 15 ml olive oil

Directions

1. Add broccoli into a food processor and pulse until finely crumbed
2. Transfer broccoli to a large sized bowl and add remaining ingredients to the bowl, mix well
3. Make small balls using the mixture and let them chill for 30 minutes
4. Place balls in your Ninja Foodi pot and Air Crisping lid
5. Let it cook for 12 minutes at 185 degrees C on the "Air Crisp" mode
6. Once done, remove and enjoy!

Nutrition Values (Per Serving) Calories: 162 Fat: 12g Carbohydrates: 2g Protein: 12g

Prep Time: 5 mins.

Cooking Time: 6 hours

Servings: 48

Ingredients:

- 24 large apples, peeled, cored and cut in chunks
- 575 ml brown sugar
- 20ml cinnamon
- 10ml nutmeg, ground
- 10ml cloves, ground
- 450 ml of water

Directions:

1. Place the pot in your Ninja Foodi according to your manual.
2. Place the Pressure Lid on your Ninja Foodi according to your manual and ensure the pressure valve is at the VENT position.
3. Put all your ingredients in the pot and stir well.
4. Cover with the lid.
5. Press "Function" and use the dial to select the "SLOW COOK" function.
6. Press "Temp" and use the dial to set the temperature to HIGH
7. Press "Time" and use the dial to set the timer to 6 hours.
8. Press the "START/STOP" button to start the cooking.
9. When done, remove from the heat and blend.
10. Serve warm.

Nutritional Values (Per Serving): *Calories: 79 Fat: 0.1g Saturated Fat: 0.1g Trans Fat: 0g Carbohydrates: 25g Fiber: 3g Sodium: 1mg Protein: 0g*

Great Brussels Bite

(Prepping time: 5 minutes\ Cooking time: 3 minutes |For 4 servings)

Ingredients

- 450g Brussels sprouts
- 60 ml pine nuts
- Salt and pepper to taste
- Olive oil as needed
- 250 ml water

Directions

1. Place a steamer basket in your Ninja Foodi and add Brussels to the basket
2. Add water and lock lid, cook on HIGH pressure for 3 minutes
3. Quick release pressure
4. Transfer Brussels to a plate and toss with olive oil, salt, pepper and sprinkle of pine nuts
5. Enjoy!

Nutrition Values (Per Serving) Calories: 112Fat: 7gCarbohydrates: 4g Protein: 5g

---

Simple Mushroom Saute

(Prepping time: 10 minutes\ Cooking time: 15 minutes |For 8 servings)

Ingredients

- 450g white mushrooms, stems trimmed
- 30 ml unsalted butter
- 2.5 ml salt
- 60 ml water

Directions

1. Quarter medium mushrooms and cut any large mushrooms into eight
2. Put mushrooms, butter, and salt in your Foodi's inner pot
3. Add water and lock pressure lid, making sure to seal the valve
4. Cook on HIGH pressure for 5 minutes, quick release pressure once did
5. Once done, set your pot to Saute mode on HIGH mode and bring the mix to a boil over 5 minutes until all the water evaporates
6. Once the butter/water has evaporated, stir for 1 minute until slightly browned
7. Enjoy!

Nutrition Values (Per Serving) *Calories: 50 Fat: 4g Carbohydrates: 2g Protein: 2g*

Delicious Assorted Nuts

(Prepping time: 5 minutes\ Cooking time: 15 minutes |For 4 servings)

Ingredients

- 15 ml butter, melted
- 125 ml raw cashew nuts
- 250 ml raw almonds
- Salt to taste

Directions

1. Add nuts to your Ninja Foodi pot
2. Lock lid and cook on "Air Crisp" mode for 10 minutes at 175 degrees C
3. Remove nuts into a bowl and add melted butter and salt
4. Toss well to coat
5. Return the mix to your Ninja Foodi, lock lid and bake for 5 minutes on BAKE/ROAST mode
6. Serve and enjoy!

Nutrition Values (Per Serving)

- Calories: 189
- Fat: 16g
- Carbohydrates: 7g
- Protein: 7g

(Prepping time: 5 minutes\ Cooking time: 17 minutes |For 4 servings)

Ingredients

- 1 spaghetti squash, halved crosswise and seeded
- 10 ml stevia
- 1.25 ml salt
- 0.5ml black pepper
- 0.5ml crushed red pepper flakes
- 50 ml unsalted butter
- 2 cloves garlic, thinly sliced
- 12 fresh sage leaves

Directions

1. Place steamer insert in your Ninja Foodi
2. Add 375 ml water to the pot
3. Place spaghetti squash halves on steamer rack and lock lid, cook on HIGH pressure for 12 minutes
4. Quick release pressure
5. Take a small bowl and add stevia, salt, pepper, pepper flakes and mix
6. Life squash out and shred using 2 forks, pour water out of pot and dry it
7. Set your pot to Saute mode and add butter, let it heat up
8. Add garlic, cook for 1 and ½ minutes
9. Add sage and stevia mixture, cook for 45 seconds
10. Pour the prepared sauce over spaghetti and stir
11. **Enjoy!**

Nutrition Values (Per Serving)

- Calories: 214
- Fat: 20g
- Carbohydrates: 5g

- Protein: 5g

Spicy Cauliflower Steak

(Prepping time: 5 minutes\ Cooking time: 5 minutes |For 4 servings)

Ingredients

- 1 large cauliflower head
- 30 ml extra virgin olive oil
- 10 ml paprika
- 10 ml ground cumin
- 3.75 ml kosher salt
- 60 ml fresh cilantro, chopped
- 1 lemon quartered

Directions

1. Place a steamer insert in your pot and add 375-ml water to the pot
2. Remove leaves form cauliflower and trim the core so the leaves sit flat
3. Transfer to rack
4. Take a small bowl and add olive oil, paprika, cumin and salt
5. Drizzle the mix over cauliflower and rub
6. Lock lid and cook on HIGH pressure for 4 minutes, quick release pressure
7. Once done, open up the lid and transfer the cooked cauliflower to a cutting board
8. Slice into 1-inch-thick steaks and divide them amongst serving plates
9. Sprinkle cilantro, serve with lemon quarters and enjoy!

Nutrition Values (Per Serving)

- Calories: 268
- Fat: 23g
- Carbohydrates: 10g
- Protein: 5g

Subtle Buffalo Chicken Meatballs

(Prepping time: 10 minutes\ Cooking time: 40 minutes |For 6 servings)

Ingredients

- 450g chicken, ground
- 1 carrot, minced
- 2 celery stalks, minced
- 60 ml blue cheese, crumbled
- 60 ml buffalo sauce (check for Keto friendliness)
- 1 whole egg
- 60 ml almond meal
- 30 ml extra virgin olive oil
- 125 ml water

Directions

1. Set your Ninja to Saute mode and set it to HIGH, let it pre-heated for 5 minutes

2. Take a large mixing bowl and add chicken, carrot, celery, blue cheese, buffalo sauce, almond meal, egg. Mix and shape the mixture into 1 and ½ inch balls

3. Pour olive oil into your pot, and add the meatballs in batches, sear until all sides are browned. Keep the seared balls on the side

4. Place Cook and Crisp Basket in the pot and add water, add the seared meatballs

5. Place pressure lid and seal the pressure valves

6. Cook on HIGH pressure for 5 minutes, quick release the pressure once did

7. Close crisping lid and cook for 10 minutes at 180 degrees C

8. After 5 minutes of cooking, open the lid and lift the basket to give it a shake, lower it back and continue cooking

9. Enjoy once done!

Nutrition Values (Per Serving)

- Calories: 204
- Fat: 13g
- Carbohydrates: 5g
- Protein: 16g

Mars Cheesecake

Prep Time: 20 mins.

Cooking Time: 2 hours

Number of Servings: 8

Ingredients:

- 340 grams cream cheese, softened
- 5 ml vanilla
- 125ml sugar + 15 ml Sugar
- 15 ml flour
- 1.25ml salt
- 2 eggs
- 250 ml sour cream
- 1 Mars bar
- 175ml graham cracker, crumbled
- 30 ml butter, melted
- 1.25ml cinnamon, ground

Directions:

1. Combine the cream cheese, the vanilla, 125ml of sugar, the salt, and the flour in a bowl.
2. Beat with a mixer on medium until smooth.
3. Add the eggs one by one, beating until combined.
4. Add the sour cream and beat until incorporated.
5. Crumble the Mars bar and add it to the mixture. Beat for half a minute then set aside.
6. In a separate bowl, mix the crumbs, the butter, 15 ml of the sugar, and the cinnamon.
7. In a springform pan that fits in your Ninja Foodi pour the crumbs mixture.

8. Press to spread on the bottom and form the crust.

9. Pour the cream cheese mixture over the crumb layer. Smooth with a spatula.

10. Add 250 ml of water in your pot and place the wire rack in it.

11. Place the springform pan on top of the rack.

12. Press "Function" and turn the dial to the "STEAM" function.

13. Press "Time" and use the dial to set it to 2 hours.

14. Press the "START/STOP" button and Close the lid to start cooking.

15. When done, allow to cool for 2 hours then place it in the refrigerator for at least 4 hours before serving.

16. Unmold by running a non-serrated knife between the cake and the pan sides.

17. Serve cold topped with caramel sauce and fun-size Mars bars.

Nutritional Values (Per Serving): *Calories: 318 Fat: 21.4g   Saturated Fat: 12.3g Trans Fat: 0.1g*
Carbohydrates: 23g   Fiber: 2g   Sodium: 592mg   Protein: 7g

Soup Recipes

Servings: 4

Preparation Time: 20 minutes

Ingredients

- 15 ml olive oil
- 3 green onions, sliced crosswise into ¼ inch pieces
- 450g asparagus, tough ends removed, cut into 1-inch pieces
- 1 litre vegetable stock
- 15 ml unsalted butter
- 15 ml almond flour
- 10ml salt
- 5 ml white pepper
- 125 ml heavy cream

Directions

1. Set your Ninja Foodi to "Sauté" mode and add oil, let it heat up
2. Add green onions and Sauté for a few minutes, add asparagus and stock
3. Lock lid and cook on HIGH pressure for 5 minutes
4. Take a small saucepan and place it over low heat, add butter, flour and stir until the mixture foams and turns into a golden beige, this is your blond roux
5. Remove from heat
6. Release pressure naturally over 10 minutes
7. Open lid and add roux, salt and pepper to the soup
8. Use an immersion blender to puree the soup
9. Taste and season accordingly, swirl in cream and enjoy!

Nutritional Information (per serving): Calories 192, Fat 14g, Carbohydrates 8g, Protein 6g.

Epic Beef Sausage Soup

Preparation time: 10 minutes

Cooking time: 30 minutes

Servings: 6

Ingredients:

- 15 ml. extra-virgin olive oil
- 1.5 litre beef broth
- 450g organic beef sausage, cooked and sliced
- 450 ml sauerkraut
- 2 celery stalks, chopped
- 1 sweet onion, chopped
- 10 ml. garlic, minced
- 30 ml. butter
- 15 ml. hot mustard
- 2.5 ml. caraway seeds
- 125 ml sour cream
- 30 ml. fresh parsley, chopped

Directions:

1. Grease the inner pot of your Ninja Foodi with olive oil.
2. Add broth, sausage, sauerkraut, celery, onion, garlic, butter, mustard, caraway seeds in the pot.
3. Lock the lid and cook on high pressure for 30 minutes.
4. Quick-release the pressure.
5. Remove the lid and stir in sour cream.
6. Serve with a topping of parsley.
7. Enjoy!

Nutrition: Calories: 165 Fat: 4 g. Carbohydrates: 14 g. Protein: 11 g.

Preparation time: 5 minutes

Cooking time: 20 minutes

Servings: 4

Ingredients:

- 750 ml fish stock
- 1 onion, diced
- 250 ml broccoli, chopped
- 450 ml celery stalks, chopped
- 375 ml cauliflower, diced
- 1 carrot, sliced
- 450g white fish fillets, chopped
- 250 ml heavy cream
- 1 bay leaf
- 30 ml. butter
- 1.25ml pepper
- 2.5 ml. salt
- 1.25ml garlic powder

Directions:

1. Set your Ninja Foodi to "Sauté" mode and add butter, let it melt.
2. Add onion and carrots, cook for 3 minutes.
3. Stir in remaining ingredients.
4. Lock the lid and cook on high pressure for 4 minutes.
5. Naturally, release the pressure over 10 minutes.
6. Discard bay leaf.
7. Serve and enjoy!

Nutrition: Calories: 298   Fat: 18 g. Carbohydrates: 6 g. Protein: 24 g.

Pressure Cooker Chicken Pot Pie Soup

Prep & Cooking time: 17 minutes

Serving 6

Ingredients

- 1 large skinless boneless chicken breast, bite-size cubed
- 1 can drained Libby's mixed vegetables
- 15 ml of olive oil
- 5 ml of garlic salt
- 15 ml minced garlic
- 1 125 ml chicken broth
- 250 ml whipping cream heavy
- 45ml of cornstarch
- 45ml chicken broth or cold water
- 1 refrigerated biscuits tube

Directions

1. Sauté chicken with garlic, olive oil, and garlic salt.
2. Then add broth and veggie mix and stir. Pressure cook for two minutes at high.
3. Add cream and mix cornstarch with water or broth. Add gradually and let it get dense for two minutes.
4. Place the biscuit dough over upside-down tin for the muffin. Bake for about 11 minutes and serve soup in them.

Nutrition Values (Per Serving)
Calories: Kcal 546 | Fat: 31g | Carbs: 52g | Protein: 16g

Prep Time: 10 mins.

Cooking Time: 20 mins.

Number of Servings: 8

Ingredients:

- To make the soup:

- 2 cloves of garlic, minced

- 60ml carrot, in small dice

- 60ml zucchini, in small dice

- 2 stalks of celery, thinly sliced

- 1/2 small onion, thinly sliced

- 450 ml broth of your preference

- 5 ml fresh basil

- 22.5 ml tomato paste

- 225g plum tomatoes, chopped

- 200g fire-roasted tomatoes, diced

- 7.5 ml olive oil

- 7.5 ml brown sugar

- salt and pepper to taste

- A pinch of chili flakes (optional)

- 52.5 ml Parmesan cheese, grated

- 30 ml flour

- 125 ml whole milk

- 30 ml butter

Directions:

1. Place the cooking pot in your Ninja Foodi according to your manual.

2. Press "Function" and turn the dial to the "Sear/Sauté" function.

3. Press "Temp" and use the dial to adjust the temperature to Medium-High.

4. Press the "START/STOP" button to start cooking.

5. Put the zucchini, the celery, the carrot, the onion, and the garlic in the pot.

6. Cook for about 5 minutes while stirring.

7. Add in the broth, the basil, the tomato paste, the two kinds of tomatoes, the olive oil, the brown sugar.

8. Season with salt and pepper to taste.

9. Close the lid and ensure the pressure valve is set to the sealed position.

10. Press FUNCTION, and turn the dial to "Pressure Cook"

11. Press "Temp" and use the dial to adjust the temperature to HIGH.

12. Press "Time" and use the dial to set the timer to 6 minutes.

13. While that is cooking, put a saucepan over low heat and melt the butter.

14. Add the flour and the milk and stir vigorously so it mixes with the butter until it's smooth.

15. When the pot is done cooking carefully turn the pressure valve to Quick Release.

16. When it releases, carefully open the lid and use an immersion blender to mash the soup.

17. Press "Function" and turn the dial to the "Sear/Sauté" function again.

18. Press "Temp" and use the dial to adjust the temperature to Medium-High.

19. Press the "START/STOP" button to start cooking.

20. Add the flour and milk mixture to the pot and stir for around 3 minutes.

21. Add in the parmesan and stir well.

22. Serve hot with toasted bread or a grilled cheese.

Nutritional Values (Per Serving): *Calories: 88 Fat: 5.1g Saturated Fat: 2.4g Trans Fat: 0.1g Carbohydrates: 9g Fiber: 1g Sodium: 321mg Protein:4g*

Conclusion

With some basic aim of teaching all the newbies excel the skill of cooking using Ninja Foodi, we have introduced some authentic, easy, and yummy recipes, that are divided into various categories; breakfast, lunch, and dinner.

After reading this guide, we hope that you will have a clear idea on how to prepare meals using Ninja Foodi. As a beginner, it's always hard to get settled with a new appliance, so this book is targeted toward all those who want to enjoy a meal prepares in Ninja Foodi.

If you follow the recipe direction provided in this book, surely you will master your cooking skills and it also has a significant effect on your overall health.

Printed in Great Britain
by Amazon

61787486R00061